MY DAD IS FANTASTIC!

HOTHOUSE

My dad is fantastic because he wakes me every morning with lovely, cuddly hugs.

"Come on," he says, "it's time to get up.
We're going to have lots of fun today."

Sometimes, when I get dressed, I put on Dad's grown-up clothes to make him laugh.

"You're far too small for those," he says.
"I think these clothes will fit you much better."

My dad is fantastic at cooking breakfast. We make a big mess, but it's great fun cracking the eggs.

"Just look at what you've done to my kitchen," says Mum,
as she folds her arms and sighs.

Me and my dad love to garden together.
We plant flower seeds and watch them grow.

Sometimes, we pretend we're fierce pirates, searching for hidden treasure.

My dad is fantastic because he builds me a tree house.
It's a secret hideaway just for us.

I help him paint it a lovely, bright orange and
I fill it with all of my best toys.

Dad teaches me how to ride my bike.
When I wibble and wobble he says, "Hold on tight."

He pushes me along and I pedal really fast,
then suddenly, I can ride all by myself!

My dad is fantastic because when I hurt myself, he picks me up and cuddles me better.

Dad carries me home on his big, strong shoulders and I can almost touch the sky.

When Dad makes me dinner, he's very silly and turns my vegetables into funny faces.

If I'm good, Dad gives me a treat.
He makes me a special, ice cream surprise.

My dad is fantastic because he makes bath time fun and fills my bath tub with floaty bubbles.

We race each other with my little toy boats
and splash water everywhere.

Later, I put on my best pyjamas and we brush our teeth until they're sparkly.

When I yawn, Dad scoops me up in his arms and says, "It's time for a bedtime story."

My dad is fantastic because he lifts me up high, so I can reach my special book.

We cuddle up and read together and
I laugh at Dad's funny voices.

When the story is over, Dad tucks me up softly and kisses me goodnight.

"Goodnight," I say, "I love you Dad.
You're fantastic!"